FOR

_____

FROM

_____

ON THE OCCASION OF

_____

DATE

_____

let's read the Gospels!

let's
read
the
Gospels

let's read the Gospels

A GUIDED JOURNAL

ANNIE F. DOWNS

Revell
a division of Baker Publishing Group
Grand Rapids, Michigan

Published by Revell
a division of Baker Publishing Group
Grand Rapids, Michigan
RevellBooks.com

Printed in China

Library of Congress Cataloging-in-Publication Data
Names: Downs, Annie F., 1980– author.
Title: Let's read the gospels : a guided journal / Annie F. Downs.
Description: Grand Rapids, Michigan : Revell, a division of Baker Publishing Group, [2024]
Identifiers: LCCN 2023018624 | ISBN 9780800745554 (cloth) | ISBN 9781493444779 (ebook)
Subjects: LCSH: Bible. Gospels—Study and teaching.
Classification: LCC BS2556 .D63 2024 | DDC 226.0071—dc23/eng/20230726
LC record available at https://lccn.loc.gov/2023018624

Interior design by William Overbeeke.

The author is represented by Alive Literary Agency, www.aliveliterary.com.

Baker Publishing Group publications use paper produced from sustainable forestry practices and post-consumer waste whenever possible.

24 25 26 27 28 29 30   7 6 5 4 3 2 1

To Johnny, Craig, Ashley, Lillian,
Cait, Lani, and Hayley.

This book is as much yours as it is mine.
Honored to do this work with you.
To God be the glory.

contents

Introduction   10

As You Read the Gospels . . .   13

GUIDED DAILY READING PLAN

introduction

Dear friend,

It's been a couple of years since this idea came to my mind—this idea to read the Gospels in a month. It's been hard for me to find a rhythm of Bible reading, so instead of trying to do a reading plan that takes a year or that goes from page alpha to page omega of the Bible, I wanted something I knew I could finish. And a plan that I figured I could finish takes a month.

I was right. I finished a month of reading the Gospels—Matthew, Mark, Luke, and John—and not only did I finish it, I really enjoyed it! So I decided to pick a different translation of the Bible and try to do it again—another thirty days in the Gospels.

It started to change my life. So I kept doing it. And after a few months, I invited my friends on social media to join me. They did. Then we created the *Let's Read the Gospels* podcast and invited friends to listen along. They did.

Over the last few years, thousands of people have read the Gospels along with me, and millions have listened to the Gospels read aloud on the *Let's Read the Gospels* podcast. It reinforced what I had already discovered for myself: reading the Gospels changes us.

This *Let's Read the Gospels* journal is designed to guide you along the same path so many of us have walked over the last few years—thirty days in the Gospels. Each day offers you a few questions to think about and journal through. Use it once, or use it over and over again. The daily reading is listed on the first page so you can read along in the Bible translation or version of your choice. If it would be easier for you to listen to the Gospels in the order that this particular journal is laid out, head to the *Let's Read the Gospels* podcast or my YouTube channel and find the recordings for April 2024.

The journal is laid out in a different order than the Bible. Instead of reading Matthew, Mark, Luke, and then John—the order in which the Bible is printed—we're going to flip it around and start with John, then Luke, on to Mark, and finish with Matthew. Starting with the book of John is a unique choice, I know. John is just such a good place to begin when we are getting in the habit of a thirty-day rhythm of reading Scripture. It moves fast, it has lots of great stories about Jesus, and it answers a lot of questions about Jesus right off the bat—even in the first day of reading! And for our friends who have read these stories a lot, flipping the order brings some new things to light. I think you're going to love it.

While I encourage you to commit to thirty days in a row (you can do it!), reading and journaling and listening along every day, I know that the reality of being human is that we miss a Wednesday or sleep in on a Saturday. So it may take you more than thirty days, and that is fine! You don't have to be in the Gospels every day to be changed, but every day you are in the Gospels will change you. So give yourself grace if you miss a day here and there, but don't give up.

I am cheering for you. I am reading right alongside you. I am certain our lives will be different by the time we finish this. Let's read the Gospels!

Sincerely,

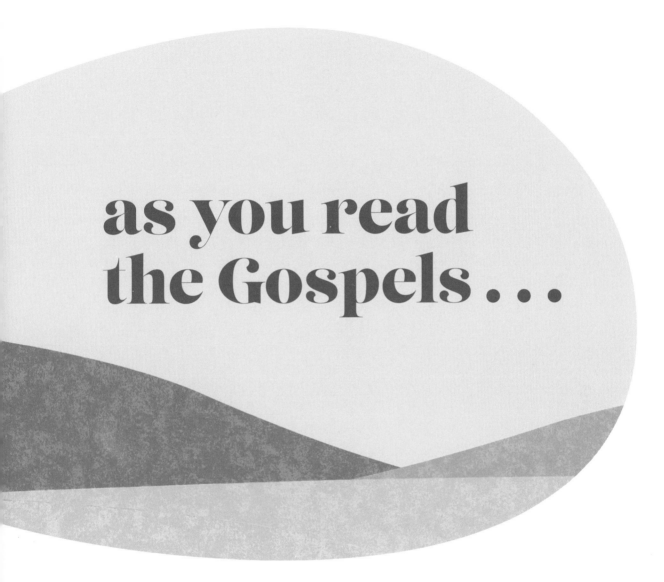

as you read
the Gospels . . .

What do you hope to learn in the next thirty days?

Why did you decide to commit to reading the Gospels for these thirty days?

Write out a short prayer—maybe one or two sentences—asking Jesus to show Himself to you in a new way this month.

Before you spend the next month reading about Him on a daily basis, what are some words you would use to describe Jesus today?

day

1

The Word became flesh and blood,
   and moved into the neighborhood.
We saw the glory with our own eyes,
   the one-of-a-kind glory,
   like Father, like Son,
Generous inside and out,
   true from start to finish.

JOHN 1:14 MSG

DAY 1

John 1–3

DATE

What did you learn about Jesus in the first paragraph of the book of John?

Jesus's first miracle was turning water into wine. Why do you think He picked that to start?

John 3:16 is probably the most well-known verse in the whole Bible. Which parts of that verse stand out to you today?

What are some characteristics you see in John the Baptist that you want to see in yourself?

DAY 1
John 1–3

DATE

What are your questions, epiphanies, and oh-wows?

day 2

READ JOHN 4–6

Then Jesus took the loaves, gave thanks to God, and distributed them to the people. Afterward he did the same with the fish. And they all ate as much as they wanted.

JOHN 6:11 NLT

Why is the story of the Samaritan woman important to you?

Today's reading is full of miracles. Which one grabbed your attention? Why?

Have you had a moment when God miraculously provided for you, like when Jesus fed the five thousand? What happened?

What are some emotions you imagine Jesus felt when His disciples began to abandon Him at the end of John 6?

What are your questions, epiphanies, and oh-wows?

day

3

When Jesus spoke again to the people, he said, "I am the light of the world. Whoever follows me will never walk in darkness, but will have the light of life."

JOHN 8:12 NIV

After the miracles of yesterday's reading, today is full of Jesus's teaching. Why do you think John wrote it in that order?

DAY 3
John 7–9

DATE

Jesus's family really struggled with His ministry. When have you faced an experience like that?

DATE

In John 7, Jesus said to come to Him if we are thirsty. Write out a short prayer telling Jesus where you are thirsty and asking Him to satisfy you.

Jesus healed multiple blind people in the Gospels. What part of this particular story in John 9 matters most to you?

DATE

What are your questions, epiphanies, and oh-wows?

day 4

READ JOHN 10–12

So the sisters sent word to Jesus, "Lord, the one you love is sick."

JOHN 11:3 NIV

DATE

Jesus is the Good Shepherd. Why does that matter to you today?

John 11:3 says, "Lord, the one you love is sick." Who are some people you would pray that for today? List them here.

What detail of Lazarus's resurrection stands out to you today? What questions is it raising for you?

What happened in John 12 was the type of entrance Jesus's followers expected to begin His reign over Jerusalem. But Jesus had a different, more painful, but far better story to tell. Have you seen that happen in your life too, where God ended up doing something that was different from your expectations? How did the story finish better than you thought it would?

What are your questions, epiphanies, and oh-wows?

day 5

Yes, I am the vine; you are the branches. Those who remain in me, and I in them, will produce much fruit. For apart from me you can do nothing.

JOHN 15:5 NLT

Who in your life serves others well, like when Jesus washed the disciples' feet? How do the people around you inspire you by the way they serve?

What do you think happened to Judas to make him turn on Jesus the way he did?

How does the promise of the Holy Spirit help you today, in the life you have right now?

God is the gardener. Jesus is the vine. You are a branch. What feelings does that raise in you today? What does it have you thinking about? How does that bring you peace? How does that speak into the purpose you feel God has for you?

DATE

What are your questions, epiphanies, and oh-wows?

day 6

I have told you these things so that in me you may have peace. You will have suffering in this world. Be courageous! I have conquered the world.

JOHN 16:33 CSB

DATE

Imagine, for a minute, John sitting right beside Jesus and hearing this whole conversation and then writing it down for us. As Jesus continued to share with His closest friends in chapters 16–17, what part do you imagine John enjoyed writing down the most?

What would it look like for believers to love each other well? What looks like love to you? What looks like love from you?

DATE

Jesus is always praying for us (Heb. 7:25). What do you hope He is praying for you today?

DATE

You will read the rest of this story—the betrayal, trial, crucifixion, death, and resurrection of Jesus—four times before this month is over. What captured you the most in John's telling of the story?

What are your questions, epiphanies, and oh-wows?

day 7

Now there are also many other things that Jesus did. Were every one of them to be written, I suppose that the world itself could not contain the books that would be written.

JOHN 21:25 ESV

DATE

What is your first thought when reading the words Pilate wrote on the sign hung at the top of Jesus's cross?

DATE

What does Jesus's death mean to you today? What emotions stir as you read this passage?

Jesus appeared to many people after His resurrection—which story matters the most to you today?

DATE

What have you learned about Jesus from John's Gospel that you didn't know before? It could be a personality trait or a statement He made or a miracle He did.

DATE

What are your questions, epiphanies, and oh-wows?

day

8

READ LUKE 1–3

His mercy flows in wave after wave
on those who are in awe before him.

LUKE 1:50 MSG

DATE

What is your favorite part of the birth story of Jesus?

Is there a line from Mary's song that you noticed in a new way today?
Copy it down here and write about why it matters to you.

Simeon and Anna were waiting for the Messiah. In what ways are you waiting for God to show up for you right now too?

Jesus's genealogy is listed here. Why do you think that is important to read in the Gospels?

What are your questions, epiphanies, and oh-wows?

day

9

READ LUKE 4–6

Jesus answered them, "It is not the healthy who need a doctor, but the sick. I have not come to call the righteous, but sinners to repentance."

LUKE 5:31-32 NIV

How does Jesus's forty days in the desert inspire you today?

DAY 9
Luke 4–6

DATE

In Luke 5, Jesus invited His first disciples to follow Him. What do you feel God is inviting you to do that will require you to walk away from something familiar?

Sabbath is mentioned a lot here. What does a day of rest look like for you?

DATE

Which of the Beatitudes did you need to read the most today? Copy it down here and then write a short prayer asking God to make that Beatitude true in your life today.

What are your questions, epiphanies, and oh-wows?

day
10

READ LUKE 7–9

What good is it for someone to gain the whole world, and yet lose or forfeit their very self?

LUKE 9:25 NIV

What do you think prompted John the Baptist's questions? What do you think about Jesus's response?

How are you inspired by the idea that Jesus's work was financially supported by the women who followed Him?

When you think of the parable of the sower, how have you seen
yourself change and grow between the different types of soil?

_____

_____

_____

_____

_____

_____

_____

_____

_____

_____

_____

_____

_____

_____

_____

_____

_____

_____

_____

_____

_____

_____

_____

_____

Today's reading is full of miracles mixed with challenging teaching.
Why do you think Luke recorded it that way?

What are your questions, epiphanies, and oh-wows?

day 11

READ LUKE 10–12

Steep yourself in God-reality, God-initiative, God-provisions. You'll find all your everyday human concerns will be met. Don't be afraid of missing out. You're my dearest friends! The Father wants to give you the very kingdom itself.

LUKE 12:31-32 MSG

Who do you relate to more—Mary or Martha? Why?

Jesus's teaching on prayer in Luke 11 is helpful and also can raise some questions. What do you wrestle with when you hear this section?

DATE

Jesus was teaching a lot in today's readings. Which verse spoke to you the loudest? Why does that matter to you today?

_____

_____

_____

_____

_____

_____

_____

_____

_____

_____

_____

_____

_____

_____

_____

_____

_____

_____

_____

_____

_____

_____

_____

DATE

In Luke 12, Jesus addressed the topic of anxiety. What are you worried about right now? How does this passage help?

What are your questions, epiphanies, and oh-wows?

day 12

And he said to him, "Son, you are always with me, and all that is mine is yours. It was fitting to celebrate and be glad, for this your brother was dead, and is alive; he was lost, and is found."

LUKE 15:31-32 ESV

DATE

What do you think about Jesus healing people on the Sabbath?

What does the "narrow way" look like to you?

DATE

In Luke 14, Jesus talked a lot about humility. Who in your life models that trait really well?

In the parable of the lost son (actually, a parable about TWO sons), which son do you more closely identify with? How does their story help you?

DATE

What are your questions, epiphanies, and oh-wows?

day
13

If you cling to your life, you will lose it, and if you let your life go, you will save it.

LUKE 17:33 NLT

DATE

The story of the persistent widow is meant to teach us to pray and not give up. What are you praying for that would be easy to give up on?

DATE

Why should we keep praying, even when we want to give up?

What emotions do you feel when you read about the rich young ruler?

A lot of today's reading is about money. What does it look like in your life to serve God but not serve money? How do we keep a balanced, faith-filled view on finances?

DATE

DATE

What are your questions, epiphanies, and oh-wows?

day

124

For the Son of Man came to seek and to save
the lost.

LUKE 19:10 NIV

DATE

What does Zacchaeus's story tell you about Jesus?

What does it look like today for you to invest the talents the Lord has given you?

Jesus said in Luke 19:46 that the temple was to be a house of prayer. What does that mean to you?

DATE

There are a lot of warnings in today's reading. Why do you think Jesus told the stories He did at the time that He did?

What are your questions, epiphanies, and oh-wows?

day 15

READ LUKE 22–24

And they worshiped him and returned to Jerusalem with great joy, and were continually in the temple blessing God.

LUKE 24:52-53 ESV

Have you participated in the Lord's Supper before? If so, what has been your favorite experience of receiving communion?

DAY 15
Luke 22–24

Jesus prayed in the garden and submitted His will to God's will. When have you submitted your will to God's in the past? Where might God be prompting you to do that now?

DATE

DATE

Someone else carried Jesus's cross for Him. What questions would you ask Simon of Cyrene about that experience?

What have you learned about Jesus from Luke that you didn't know before?

DATE

What are your questions, epiphanies, and oh-wows?

day
16

READ MARK 1–3

And a voice came from heaven: "You are my Son, whom I love; with you I am well pleased."

MARK 1:11 NIV

Mark jumps in right away with Jesus's life and ministry by telling the story of His baptism. What is your baptism story? (If you haven't been baptized yet, what is factoring into that decision?)

DATE

The paralyzed man was brought to Jesus through the roof by his friends. When have your friends sacrificed for you in that way—caring for you when you couldn't care for yourself?

What are your thoughts about fasting? Have you ever fasted? Why do you think Jesus talked about fasting as much as He did?

How have you seen a "house divided" scenario play out in your family, in your life, or in your country? What was the result?

What are your questions, epiphanies, and oh-wows?

day

17

READ MARK 4–6

When Jesus overheard what was said, he told the synagogue leader, "Don't be afraid. Only believe."

MARK 5:36 CSB

Jesus talked in Mark 4 about secrets coming out into the open. What is the benefit of not having secrets in your life? Think about what's hidden or secret for you right now. What would it take for you to let Jesus bring that into the light?

DATE

DATE

Today's reading is full of miracles. Which is your favorite? Why?

Imagine the scene at Herod's party. What might you be feeling if you were in attendance?

We're reading story after story of Jesus healing people by their faith and His touch. What healing do you need from Jesus?

DATE

What are your questions, epiphanies, and oh-wows?

READ MARK 7–9

Immediately the father of the child cried out and said, "I believe; help my unbelief!"

MARK 9:24 ESV

Jesus healed a few different men in this section of reading. How are the healings different? How do they seem similar?

DATE

What does it mean for you that Jesus healed different people in different ways?

In Mark 8:35, Jesus said, "For whoever wants to save their life will lose it, but whoever loses their life for me and for the gospel will save it." What does that mean to you? What does that look like for you?

DATE

"I believe; help my unbelief!" Have you ever prayed a prayer kind of like that? In what situations or areas of your life do you pray this way?

What are your questions, epiphanies, and oh-wows?

day

19

Looking at them, Jesus said, "With man it is impossible, but not with God, because all things are possible with God."

MARK 10:27 CSB

DATE

What does it mean to receive the kingdom of God like a child?

DATE

Jesus said that with God, all things are possible. What feels impossible in your life right now?

Jesus asked the blind man, "What do you want me to do for you?"
What do you want Jesus to do for you?

How can you practice loving your neighbor as yourself? How are you practicing loving yourself?

What are your questions, epiphanies, and oh-wows?

day
20

Keep watch and pray, so that you will not give in to temptation. For the spirit is willing, but the body is weak.

MARK 14:38 NLT

What does it look like to stay alert for Jesus's return?

Just like the woman with the bottle of perfume, how can you make a beautiful offering to Jesus in your life?

This is your third time reading about the last week of Jesus's life.
What in particular stands out to you from Mark's version?

With only one last chapter to read in Mark, what have you learned about Jesus from this book that you didn't know before? What details or stories have stood out to you?

DATE

What are your questions, epiphanies, and oh-wows?

day 21

READ MARK 16;
MATTHEW 1–2

When Joseph woke from sleep, he did as the angel of the Lord commanded him.

MATTHEW 1:24 ESV

DATE

Why is it important to you that, after His resurrection, Jesus appeared first to Mary Magdalene?

DATE

Today's reading takes you from Jesus's ascension back to His birth. What are you experiencing in that transition?

DATE

Joseph accepted Jesus as his own son. Have you been accepted by a mentor, stepparent, or another adult who cared for you when they didn't have to? How are you better for it?

DATE

The star actually led the magi to Jerusalem before it led them to Bethlehem. When they obeyed, it took them to the seemingly wrong place. In what ways does this experience feel familiar to you?

DATE

What are your questions, epiphanies, and oh-wows?

day 22

READ MATTHEW 3–5

Jesus answered, "It is written: 'Man shall not live on bread alone, but on every word that comes from the mouth of God.'"

MATTHEW 4:4 NIV

In Matthew 3:16–17, God the Father told Jesus that He was pleased before Jesus ever did a day of ministry. Why does this matter to you?

In what ways have you felt tempted by Satan to take care of yourself or provide for yourself?

DATE

Jesus said you are blessed when people insult you because of Him.
How does that bring you peace today?

Jesus taught a lot about how sin isn't just what we do on the outside; sin can be in our hearts and minds as well. This is a safe place to examine your heart and mind. What is God saying to you about them today?

DATE

DATE

What are your questions, epiphanies, and oh-wows?

day 23

Ask, and it will be given to you. Seek, and you will find. Knock, and the door will be opened to you. For everyone who asks receives, and the one who seeks finds, and to the one who knocks, the door will be opened.

MATTHEW 7:7-8 CSB

DATE

What does it mean to you to store up treasures in heaven?

DATE

What would it look like to continue to ask, seek, and knock for the prayers you are praying right now?

Jesus talked about the cost of following Him. How have you experienced that in your life?

What storm in your life would you like Jesus to calm?

What are your questions, epiphanies, and oh-wows?

day

24

When he saw the crowds, he had compassion for
them, because they were harassed and helpless,
like sheep without a shepherd.

MATTHEW 9:36 ESV

Jesus heals and forgives. Why does that combination seem powerful to you?

A twelve-year-old girl was brought back to life and healed. A woman was healed of her condition after bleeding for twelve years. Why does that combination seem powerful to you?

DATE

Jesus healed blind and mute people in the same story. Why does that combination seem powerful to you?

DATE

Jesus sent His disciples out in groups of two instead of sending them alone. Why does that combination seem powerful to you?

What are your questions, epiphanies, and oh-wows?

day
25

READ MATTHEW 12–14

As for what was sown on good soil, this is the one who hears the word and understands it. He indeed bears fruit and yields, in one case a hundredfold, in another sixty, and in another thirty.

MATTHEW 13:23 ESV

DATE

A good tree bears good fruit. Who in your life comes to mind when you think of someone who bears good fruit? What does that look like?

DATE

Jesus so often taught through parables. Do stories connect better with you than lessons? Why do you think that is the case?

DATE

Where are you sowing seeds right now, hoping that God will grow something there?

_____
_____
_____
_____
_____
_____
_____
_____
_____
_____
_____
_____
_____
_____
_____
_____
_____
_____
_____
_____
_____
_____
_____
_____
_____

DATE

Like Peter, have you ever had a "walking on water" moment with Jesus? When were you invited to be brave beyond what you thought you could do?

DATE

What are your questions, epiphanies, and oh-wows?

day

26

Simon Peter replied, "You are the Christ, the Son of the living God."

MATTHEW 16:16 ESV

How has Jesus provided for you in a miraculous way?

When yeast gets mixed into bread dough, the bread expands. When have you seen that same principle—whether it was gossip or lies or even kindness—play out in your life or community?

DATE

Jesus predicted His death over and over in the Gospels. Why do you think He wanted to give the disciples a heads-up about the future?

DATE _____

In Matthew 17, Peter had an experience with Jesus that he didn't want to end. When have you felt that way before?

_____

_____

_____

_____

_____

_____

_____

_____

_____

_____

_____

_____

_____

_____

_____

_____

_____

_____

_____

_____

_____

_____

_____

_____

_____

What are your questions, epiphanies, and oh-wows?

day 27

That is what the Son of Man has done: He came to serve, not be served—and then to give away his life in exchange for the many who are held hostage.

MATTHEW 20:28 MSG

DAY 27
Matthew 18–20

DATE
_____

The disciples tended to argue a bit here and there. Their humanness is helpful when we think of our own lives. How does it help you today?

_____
_____
_____
_____
_____
_____
_____
_____
_____
_____
_____
_____
_____
_____
_____
_____
_____
_____
_____
_____
_____
_____

Jesus said He'll leave the ninety-nine to pursue the one. When have you felt like the one? When have you experienced Jesus pursuing you?

DATE

_____

Why do you think Jesus said it's hard for a rich person to get into heaven?

_____

_____

_____

_____

_____

_____

_____

_____

_____

_____

_____

_____

_____

_____

_____

_____

_____

_____

_____

_____

_____

_____

_____

DATE

The parable at the beginning of Matthew 20 can feel complicated.
Does it to you? In what ways?

DATE

What are your questions, epiphanies, and oh-wows?

day 28

Jesus replied: "Love the Lord your God with all your heart and with all your soul and with all your mind."

MATTHEW 22:37 NIV

DATE

What does it look like for you to love the Lord with your whole heart?

DATE

What does it look like for you to love the Lord with your whole soul?

DATE

What does it look like for you to love the Lord with your whole mind?

DATE

Jesus warns against hypocrisy. Where might you need to examine the disconnects between what you do and what you believe?

What are your questions, epiphanies, and oh-wows?

day
29

And the King will answer them, "Truly, I say to you, as you did it to one of the least of these my brothers, you did it to me."

MATTHEW 25:40 ESV

What would it mean to hear God say to you, "Well done, good and faithful servant"?

The disciples sang a hymn together. What worship songs or hymns are you loving right now?

DATE

This is your fourth time reading about what happened in the garden of Gethsemane. What new details do you notice in Matthew's account?

The story of Peter denying Christ is heartbreaking. Reflect on what you have felt as you've read this part of the story over and over in these four books.

DATE

What are your questions, epiphanies, and oh-wows?

day 30

Jesus, undeterred, went right ahead and gave his charge: "God authorized and commanded me to commission you: Go out and train everyone you meet, far and near, in this way of life, marking them by baptism in the threefold name: Father, Son, and Holy Spirit. Then instruct them in the practice of all I have commanded you. I'll be with you as you do this, day after day after day, right up to the end of the age."

MATTHEW 28:18-20 MSG

DATE

How has Jesus's resurrection changed your life?

DATE

What does it look like to follow the Great Commission and make disciples in your life?

Why do you think Matthew recorded these last words of Jesus for us?

DATE

What have you learned about Jesus from Matthew that you didn't know before? What details or stories have stood out to you?

What are your questions, epiphanies, and oh-wows?

conclusion

Dear friend,

And here we are. Thirty (or so) days later, and you've finished. Well done to you! I bet you are able to identify a few ways that you are clearly different and better for the experience. But I bet there are ways that you have not even discovered yet. Sometime in the next few weeks, someone may ask a question about prayer, and your mind will go back to the Lord's Prayer, and you'll remember where you were when you read it or heard it. A television program will show a garden growing, and you'll think of the parable of the sower and what happens when all the seeds land in different soils. You may not remember the story exactly (I don't either), so you'll open up Matthew 13 and read it again. You'll realize one of the best parts of being in Scripture: Scripture is now in you too.

We tend to always read from front to back . . . in order, you know? Matthew, Mark, Luke, then John. But you can choose your own adventure! Since all the readings are listed at the front of the book, you can read them in any order you like! You can journal in these pages or reflect in a separate journal. In fact, we've also included a couple of other reading plans in case you'd like to take a different path through the Gospels the next time you read them.

And if you're ready to venture further into the New Testament or to try a topical Bible study, I encourage you to do that. The writer of Hebrews tells us that "the word of God is living and active" (Heb. 4:12). Whichever plan you follow or path you choose, when you spend time in Scripture, God meets you there!

He doesn't have any limits. It's one of my favorite things to remember because it reminds us how much we can trust Him. It's like what the last few words of the Gospel of John say: "Jesus did many other things as well. If every one of them were written down, I suppose that even the whole world would not have room for the books that would be written" (21:25 NIV). That verse always makes me teary—thinking of all we will learn for eternity! There are so many more ways for us to know Jesus. So many more things for us to discover with Him. Let's keep asking, seeking, and knocking so we can know Him and follow Him. Wanna do it all again? Yeah, me too.

Let's read the Gospels. Again and again.

Sincerely,
Annie

You don't have to be in the Gospels every day to be changed, but every day you are in the Gospels will change you.

How has your life been impacted by being in the Gospels for thirty days?

What are some words you would use to describe Jesus now that you have read all the way through the four Gospels?

Look back at days 7, 15, 21, and 30, and record what you learned about Jesus from each book.

John

Luke

Mark

Matthew

Think about the ways Jesus showed Himself to you through the Gospels. What do you want to say to Him?

Write out a short prayer here—maybe one or two sentences—thanking Jesus for showing Himself to you in new ways this month.

an invitation

As you've spent this month in the story of Jesus, you may have realized that you have known ABOUT Him without ever getting to KNOW Him—asking Him to forgive you and choosing to follow Him with your life. If that's something you want to do, there's no need to wait! You can tell Him that right now. Simply pray something like this:

Jesus, I believe that You are who You say You are. Please forgive me for the ways I've chosen a different path than the one that keeps me connected to You. I want to follow You and be Yours. Please help me follow You every day. Amen.

If you just prayed that prayer, CONGRATULATIONS! I'm SO happy for you . . . WITH you! What an amazing step, beginning a relationship with Jesus. Something I like to say is that He saved me once, but He rescues me all the time. He wants to do that for you too!

A great next step is to share your decision with someone in your up-close life or someone at a local church. Another important step to take is to follow Jesus's example of being baptized. It's a symbol of identifying with Him—with His death, burial, and resurrection—and it's a public way to share that you've decided you want IN on the abundant life, hope, and redemption that a relationship with God offers. Share your desire to be baptized with someone at church. I promise they will be SO excited for you and they'll help you with all the ins and outs of the process.

alternate reading plans

Since the pages of this journal are not dated, you can use them multiple times, and you can use them to approach the Gospels in a variety of orders! We LOVE options, right?! On the following pages are some alternate reading plans to get you started, or you can chart your own path. The questions may not match up perfectly, but that's okay. The important thing is to keep reading, keep asking questions, keep praying, and keep getting to know Jesus. Remember, you don't have to spend every day in the Gospels to be changed, but every day you spend in the Gospels WILL change you.

Day	In three chapters a day in the order they appear canonically	In two to four chapters a day, keeping daily readings within the same book	In the order of when scholars think they were written	Beginning with Luke, who tells the most familiar story of Jesus's birth
1	☐ Matthew 1–3	☐ Matthew 1–3	☐ Mark 1–3	☐ Luke 1–3
2	☐ Matthew 4–6	☐ Matthew 4–6	☐ Mark 4–7	☐ Luke 4–6
3	☐ Matthew 7–9	☐ Matthew 7–9	☐ Mark 8–10	☐ Luke 7–9
4	☐ Matthew 10–12	☐ Matthew 10–12	☐ Mark 11–13	☐ Luke 10–12
5	☐ Matthew 13–15	☐ Matthew 13–15	☐ Mark 14–16	☐ Luke 13–15
6	☐ Matthew 16–18	☐ Matthew 16–18	☐ Matthew 1–3	☐ Luke 16–18
7	☐ Matthew 19–21	☐ Matthew 19–21	☐ Matthew 4–6	☐ Luke 19–21
8	☐ Matthew 22–24	☐ Matthew 22–24	☐ Matthew 7–9	☐ Luke 22–24
9	☐ Matthew 25–27	☐ Matthew 25–26	☐ Matthew 10–12	☐ John 1–3
10	☐ Matthew 28, Mark 1–2	☐ Matthew 27–28	☐ Matthew 13–15	☐ John 4–6
11	☐ Mark 3–5	☐ Mark 1–3	☐ Matthew 16–18	☐ John 7–9
12	☐ Mark 6–8	☐ Mark 4–7	☐ Matthew 19–21	☐ John 10–12
13	☐ Mark 9–11	☐ Mark 8–10	☐ Matthew 22–24	☐ John 13–15
14	☐ Mark 12–14	☐ Mark 11–13	☐ Matthew 25–26	☐ John 16–18
15	☐ Mark 15–16, Luke 1	☐ Mark 14–16	☐ Matthew 27–28	☐ John 19–21

Day	In three chapters a day in the order they appear canonically	In two to four chapters a day, keeping daily readings within the same book	In the order of when scholars think they were written	Beginning with Luke, who tells the most familiar story of Jesus's birth
16	☐ Luke 2–4	☐ Luke 1–3	☐ Luke 1–3	☐ Mark 1–3
17	☐ Luke 5–7	☐ Luke 4–6	☐ Luke 4–6	☐ Mark 4–7
18	☐ Luke 8–10	☐ Luke 7–9	☐ Luke 7–9	☐ Mark 8–10
19	☐ Luke 11–13	☐ Luke 10–12	☐ Luke 10–12	☐ Mark 11–13
20	☐ Luke 14–16	☐ Luke 13–15	☐ Luke 13–15	☐ Mark 14–16
21	☐ Luke 17–19	☐ Luke 16–18	☐ Luke 16–18	☐ Matthew 1–3
22	☐ Luke 20–22	☐ Luke 19–21	☐ Luke 19–21	☐ Matthew 4–6
23	☐ Luke 23–24, John 1	☐ Luke 22–24	☐ Luke 22–24	☐ Matthew 7–9
24	☐ John 2–4	☐ John 1–3	☐ John 1–3	☐ Matthew 10–12
25	☐ John 5–7	☐ John 4–6	☐ John 4–6	☐ Matthew 13–15
26	☐ John 8–10	☐ John 7–9	☐ John 7–9	☐ Matthew 16–18
27	☐ John 11–13	☐ John 10–12	☐ John 10–12	☐ Matthew 19–21
28	☐ John 14–16	☐ John 13–15	☐ John 13–15	☐ Matthew 22–24
29	☐ John 17–19	☐ John 16–18	☐ John 16–18	☐ Matthew 25–26
30	☐ John 20–21	☐ John 19–21	☐ John 19–21	☐ Matthew 27–28

Let's Read the Gospels Chronologically

Day	Readings	☑
1	Mark 1:1a	☐
	Luke 1:1–4	☐
	John 1:1–18	☐
	Matthew 1:1–17	☐
	Luke 3:23b–38	☐
	Luke 1:5–38	☐
2	Luke 1:39–80	☐
	Matthew 1:18–25	☐
	Luke 2:1–40	☐
	Matthew 2	☐
3	Luke 2:41–52	☐
	Mark 1:1b–8	☐
	Matthew 3:1–12	☐
	Luke 3:1–18	☐
	Mark 1:9–11	☐
	Matthew 3:13–17	☐
	Luke 3:21–22	☐
	Mark 1:12–13	☐
	Matthew 4:1–11	☐
	Luke 4:1–15	☐
	John 1:19–34	☐

Day	Readings	☑
4	John 1:35–51	☐
	John 2–3	☐
	John 4:1–45	☐
	Luke 3:19–20	☐
5	Mark 1:14–15	☐
	Matthew 4:12–17	☐
	Luke 3:23a	☐
	John 4:46–54	☐
	Luke 4:16–30	☐
	Mark 1:16–20	☐
	Matthew 4:18–22	☐
	Mark 1:21–28	☐
	Luke 4:31–37	☐
	Mark 1:29–34	☐
	Matthew 8:14–17	☐
	Luke 4:38–41	☐
	Mark 1:35–39	☐
	Luke 4:42–44	☐
	Matthew 4:23–25	☐
	Luke 5:1–11	☐
	Mark 1:40–45	☐

Day	Readings	☑
	Matthew 8:1–4	☐
	Luke 5:12–16	☐
6	Mark 2:1–12	☐
	Matthew 9:1–8	☐
	Luke 5:17–26	☐
	Mark 2:13–17	☐
	Matthew 9:9–13	☐
	Luke 5:27–32	☐
	Mark 2:18–22	☐
	Matthew 9:14–17	☐
	Luke 5:33–39	☐
	John 5	☐
	Mark 2:23–28	☐
	Matthew 12:1–8	☐
	Luke 6:1–5	☐
	Mark 3:1–6	☐
	Matthew 12:9–14	☐
	Luke 6:6–11	☐
	Matthew 12:15–21	☐
7	Mark 3:7–19	☐
	Luke 6:12–16	☐
	Matthew 5:1–12	☐
	Luke 6:17–26	☐
	Matthew 5:13–48	☐

Day	Readings	☑
	Luke 6:27–36	☐
	Matthew 6:1–34	☐
8	Matthew 7:1–6	☐
	Luke 6:37–42	☐
	Matthew 7:7–20	☐
	Luke 6:43–45	☐
	Matthew 7:21–29	☐
	Luke 6:46–49	☐
	Matthew 8:5–13	☐
	Luke 7:1–17	☐
	Matthew 11:1–19	☐
	Luke 7:18–35	☐
9	Matthew 11:20–30	☐
	Luke 7:36–50	☐
	Luke 8:1–3	☐
	Mark 3:20–30	☐
	Matthew 12:22–45	☐
	Mark 3:31–35	☐
	Matthew 12:46–50	☐
	Luke 8:19–21	☐
	Mark 4:1–9	☐
	Matthew 13:1–9	☐
	Luke 8:4–8	☐
	Mark 4:10–20	☐

Day	Readings	☑
	Matthew 13:10–23	☐
	Luke 8:9–15	☐
10	Luke 8:16–18	☐
	Mark 4:21–29	☐
	Matthew 13:24–30	☐
	Mark 4:30–34	☐
	Matthew 13:31–52	☐
	Mark 4:35–41	☐
	Matthew 8:23–27	☐
	Luke 8:22–25	☐
	Mark 5:1–20	☐
	Matthew 8:28–34	☐
	Luke 8:26–39	☐
11	Mark 5:21–43	☐
	Matthew 9:18–26	☐
	Luke 8:40–56	☐
	Matthew 9:27–34	☐
	Mark 6:1–6	☐
	Matthew 13:53–58	☐
	Matthew 9:35–38	☐
	Mark 6:7–13	☐
	Matthew 10:1–42	☐
	Luke 9:1–6	☐
12	Luke 9:7–9	☐
	Mark 6:14–29	☐

Day	Readings	☑
	Matthew 14:1–21	☐
	Mark 6:30–44	☐
	Luke 9:10–17	☐
	John 6:1–15	☐
	Mark 6:45–52	☐
	Matthew 14:22–33	☐
	John 6:16–21	☐
	Mark 6:53–56	☐
	Matthew 14:34–36	☐
	John 6:22–71	☐
13	Mark 7:1–23	☐
	Matthew 15:1–20	☐
	Mark 7:24–30	☐
	Matthew 15:21–28	☐
	Mark 7:31–37	☐
	Matthew 15:29–31	☐
	Mark 8:1–10	☐
	Matthew 15:32–39	☐
	Matthew 16:1–4	☐
	Mark 8:11–21	☐
	Matthew 16:5–12	☐
14	Mark 8:22–30	☐
	Matthew 16:13–20	☐
	Luke 9:18–20	☐
	Mark 8:31–9:1	☐

Day	Readings	☑
	Matthew 16:21–28	☐
	Luke 9:21–27	☐
	Mark 9:2–13	☐
	Matthew 17:1–13	☐
	Luke 9:28–36	☐
	Mark 9:14–29	☐
	Matthew 17:14–21	☐
	Luke 9:37–43	☐
	Mark 9:30–32	☐
	Matthew 17:22–23	☐
	Luke 9:43–45	☐
	Matthew 17:24–27	☐
15	Mark 9:33–37	☐
	Matthew 18:1–6	☐
	Luke 9:46–48	☐
	Mark 9:38–41	☐
	Luke 9:49–50	☐
	Mark 9:42–50	☐
	Matthew 18:7–10	☐
	Matthew 18:12–35	☐
	John 7:1–9	☐
	Luke 9:51–56	☐
	Matthew 8:18–22	☐
	Luke 9:57–62	☐
	John 7:10–53	☐

Day	Readings	☑
16	John 8	☐
	Luke 10	☐
	Luke 11:1–13	☐
17	Luke 11:14–54	☐
	Luke 12	☐
	Luke 13:1–21	☐
	John 9	☐
18	John 10	☐
	Luke 13:22–35	☐
	Luke 14	☐
	Luke 15	☐
19	Luke 16	☐
	Luke 17:1–10	☐
	John 11	☐
	Luke 17:11–37	☐
	Luke 18:1–8	☐
20	Luke 18:9–14	☐
	Mark 10:1–12	☐
	Matthew 19:1–12	☐
	Mark 10:13–16	☐
	Matthew 19:13–15	☐
	Luke 18:15–17	☐
	Mark 10:17–31	☐
	Matthew 19:16–30	☐
	Luke 18:18–30	☐

Day	Readings	☑
	Matthew 20:1–16	☐
	Mark 10:32–34	☐
	Matthew 20:17–19	☐
	Luke 18:31–34	☐
	Mark 10:35–45	☐
	Matthew 20:20–28	☐
21	Matthew 20:29–34	☐
	Mark 10:46–52	☐
	Luke 18:35–43	☐
	Luke 19:1–27	☐
	Mark 14:3–9	☐
	Matthew 26:6–13	☐
	John 12:1–11	☐
	Mark 11:1–11	☐
	Matthew 21:1–11	☐
	Luke 19:28–40	☐
	John 12:12–19	☐
	Luke 19:41–44	☐
22	John 12:20–50	☐
	Mark 11:12–14	☐
	Matthew 21:18–22	☐
	Mark 11:15–19	☐
	Matthew 21:12–17	☐
	Luke 19:45–48	☐
	Mark 11:20–33	☐

Day	Readings	☑
	Matthew 21:23–27	☐
	Luke 20:1–8	☐
	Matthew 21:28–32	☐
	Mark 12:1–12	☐
	Matthew 21:33–46	☐
	Luke 20:9–19	☐
23	Matthew 22:1–14	☐
	Mark 12:13–17	☐
	Matthew 22:15–22	☐
	Luke 20:20–26	☐
	Mark 12:18–27	☐
	Matthew 22:23–33	☐
	Luke 20:27–40	☐
	Mark 12:28–34	☐
	Matthew 22:34–40	☐
	Mark 12:35–37	☐
	Matthew 22:41–46	☐
	Luke 20:41–44	☐
	Mark 12:38–40	☐
	Matthew 23:1–12	☐
	Luke 20:45–47	☐
	Matthew 23:13–39	☐
	Mark 12:41–44	☐
	Luke 21:1–4	☐

Day	Readings	☑
24	Mark 13:1–23	☐
	Matthew 24:1–25	☐
	Luke 21:5–24	☐
	Mark 13:24–31	☐
	Matthew 24:26–35	☐
	Luke 21:25–33	☐
	Mark 13:32–37	☐
	Matthew 24:36–51	☐
	Luke 21:34–38	☐
	Matthew 25:1–13	☐
25	Matthew 25:14–46	☐
	Mark 14:1–2	☐
	Matthew 26:1–5	☐
	Luke 22:1–2	☐
	Mark 14:10–11	☐
	Matthew 26:14–16	☐
	Luke 22:3–6	☐
	Mark 14:12–16	☐
	Matthew 26:17–19	☐
	Luke 22:7–13	☐
	John 13:1–17	☐
	Mark 14:17–26	☐
	Matthew 26:20–30	☐
	Luke 22:14–30	☐
	John 13:18–30	☐

Day	Readings	☑
26	John 13:31–38	☐
	Mark 14:27–31	☐
	Matthew 26:31–35	☐
	Luke 22:31–38	☐
	John 14–17	☐
27	John 18:1–2	☐
	Mark 14:32–42	☐
	Matthew 26:36–46	☐
	Luke 22:39–46	☐
	Mark 14:43–52	☐
	Matthew 26:47–56	☐
	Luke 22:47–53	☐
	John 18:3–24	☐
	Mark 14:53–65	☐
	Matthew 26:57–68	☐
	Mark 14:66–72	☐
	Matthew 26:69–75	☐
	Luke 22:54–62	☐
	John 18:25–27	☐
28	Mark 15:1	☐
	Matthew 27:1–2	☐
	Luke 22:66–71	☐
	Matthew 27:3–10	☐
	Mark 15:2–5	☐
	Matthew 27:11–14	☐

Day	Readings	☑
	Luke 23:1–12	☐
	John 18:28–40	☐
	Mark 15:6–15	☐
	Matthew 27:15–26	☐
	Luke 23:13–25	☐
	John 19:1–16	☐
	Mark 15:16–20	☐
	Matthew 27:27–31	☐
	Luke 22:63–65	☐
29	Mark 15:21–24	☐
	Matthew 27:32–34	☐
	Luke 23:26–31	☐
	John 19:17	☐
	Mark 15:25–32	☐
	Matthew 27:35–44	☐
	Luke 23:32–43	☐
	John 19:18–27	☐
	Mark 15:33–41	☐
	Matthew 27:45–56	☐
	Luke 23:44–49	☐
	John 19:28–37	☐
	Mark 15:42–47	☐

Day	Readings	☑
	Matthew 27:57–61	☐
	Luke 23:50–56	☐
	John 19:38–42	☐
	Matthew 27:62–66	☐
30	Mark 16:1–8	☐
	Matthew 28:1–7	☐
	Luke 24:1–12	☐
	Mark 16:9–11	☐
	John 20:1–18	☐
	Matthew 28:8–15	☐
	Luke 24:13–43	☐
	Mark 16:12–13	☐
	John 20:19–23	☐
	Mark 16:14	☐
	John 20:24–31	☐
	John 21:1–23	☐
	Matthew 28:16–20	☐
	Mark 16:15–18	☐
	Luke 24:44–49	☐
	Mark 16:19–20	☐
	Luke 24:50–53	☐
	John 21:24–25	☐

acknowledgments

I'm grateful beyond measure to get to do this work, to spend time in the Gospels and invite so many readers and listeners and friends along for the ride.

Thank you to the team at Revell for believing in this project with us and making our dreams even bigger for what this could be and how it could impact lives. And thanks to Lisa Jackson, my literary agent, for always joining us in the work we all believe matters most.

Thank you to the That Sounds Fun Network for going above and beyond to get the *Let's Read the Gospels* podcast to so many ears and hearts. Thank you to KCH Management for walking alongside this project and helping it become a reality. Thank you to the Downs Books Inc. team for pouring your hearts and time into sharing the Gospels. I'm so grateful you are here.

To our listener friends, we love making things for you. We love it MOST when it makes us all more like Jesus. Thank you for loving what we love and loving what we make. We will keep going.

To Jesus. You saved me once, but You rescue me all the time. This is all for You. You are the reason.

Annie F. Downs is a *New York Times* bestselling author, sought-after speaker, and successful podcast host based in Nashville, Tennessee. Engaging and honest, she makes readers and listeners alike feel as if they've been longtime friends. Founder of the That Sounds Fun Network—which includes her aptly named flagship show, *That Sounds Fun*—and author of multiple bestselling books like *That Sounds Fun*, *What Sounds Fun to You?*, *Chase the Fun*, *100 Days to Brave*, and *Remember God*, Annie shoots straight and doesn't shy away from the tough topics. But she always finds her way back to the truth that God is good and that life is a gift. Annie is a huge fan of laughing with friends, confetti, soccer, and boiled peanuts (preferably from a backroads Georgia gas station). Read more at AnnieFDowns.com and find her (embarrassingly easily) all over the internet @AnnieFDowns.